WILD about
EMERGENCY VEHICLES

By Caroline Bingham

*Technical Consultants: Keith Faulkner of Jane's Defence Weekly
and Peter Symons of Ice Marketing*

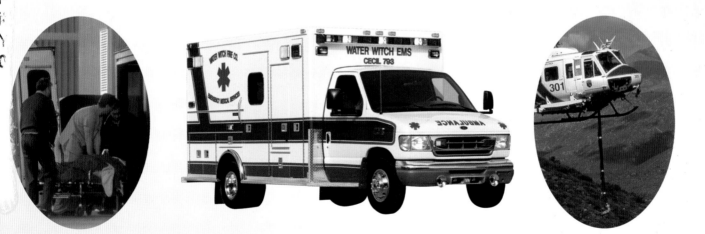

Stats and Facts • Top makes • Top models • Top speeds

WILD about
EMERGENCY VEHICLES

Copyright © *ticktock* Entertainment Ltd 2003
First published in Great Britain in 2003 by *ticktock* Media Ltd.,
Unit 2, Orchard Business Centre, North Farm Road, Tunbridge Wells, Kent, TN2 3XF
We would like to thank: Tim Bones and Elizabeth Wiggans.
Picture Credits: Alamy: P9b, P19t, P26-27c. Bronto: P1bl, P6-7. Check-6 images: P1cr, P8-9c, P14-15, P26c. Jane's Defence Weekly: P28-29c. London Fire Authority: P19-20c. Oshkosh: P3bl, P4-5, P10-11, P31b. Perry Slingsby Systems: P3br, P24-25c, P30b. RNLI: P20-21. Robinson Helicopters: P12-13. Sylvia Corday Photo Library: P25t. US Coastguard: P2, P16-17, P22-23, P29t, P30t.
ISBN 978 1 86007 366 3
Printed in China
A CIP catalogue record for this book is available from the British Library.

CONTENTS

STRIKER 4500 FIRE ENGINE

The Striker 4500 is a giant fire engine used to tackle airport fires. It is the largest fire engine in the world. The Striker has a massive water **tank** that can hold as much water as nine ordinary fire engines.

The Striker has giant wheels. They lift the **body** off the ground so the Striker can drive over muddy ground easily and get to the scene of a fire as quickly as possible.

The Striker has a special tool called a Snozzle on the end of its **arm**. If an aircraft catches fire, the Snozzle pierces a hole in its body and a camera on the end looks inside.

The snozzle then squirts in foam to put out the fire.

The sprayers are controlled by a joystick inside the **cab**.

BRONTO SKYLIFT FIRE TRUCK

DID YOU KNOW?

The Bronto's platform can also be used like a crane. It can lift a casualty on a stretcher out of a building.

The Bronto Skylift has the longest **aerial platform** in the world. This fire engine is used to tackle fires in very tall buildings. It can reach up and rescue people on the 33rd floor of a skyscraper.

BRONTO SKYLIFT F 88 HLA

ABOVE

Bronto have broken several height records with their aerial platform fire engines. This latest model can reach 72 metres into the air.

LAUNCHED: *2000*

ORIGIN: *Finland*

MAX POWER: *480 bhp*

LENGTH: *15 metres*

WIDTH: *2.5 metres*

HEIGHT: *3.9 metres*

MAX SPEED: *40 mph*

FUEL CAPACITY: *265 litres*

WATER DISCHARGE CAPACITY: *3,800 litres per minute*

ROTATION: *360°*

MAX LOAD: *400 kg*

WEIGHT: *47.5 tonnes*

CREW: *5*

COST: *£232,000*

The Bronto has a thick steel **hose**. It unfolds with the steel **boom** (arm) when the Skylift is called into action.

The aerial platform can be controlled by the firefighter on the platform, or from the ground.

HEAVY RESCUE 56 TRUCK

This amazing vehicle is owned by the Los Angeles Fire Department. It is called to accidents that need cutting or heavy lifting. The Heavy Rescue 56 is used to help out at emergencies from traffic accidents to collapsed buildings.

The **boom** can be swung to the side to lift a vehicle out of a ditch or a river.

DID YOU KNOW?

In dangerous situations, the Heavy Rescue's lifting boom can be operated by remote control – from 152 metres away if necessary!

Legs called **outriggers** steady the truck as the **winch** is raised. Each outrigger can be moved if the vehicle is on uneven ground.

STATS AND FACTS

LAUNCHED: *1995*

ORIGIN: *USA*

MAX POWER: *460 bhp*

LENGTH: *10 metres*

WIDTH: *3 metres*

HEIGHT: *3.5 metres*

MAX SPEED: *100 mph*

FUEL CAPACITY: *299 litres*

MAX LOAD: *36.2 tonnes*

WEIGHT: *2.2 tonnes*

GEARS: *18 forward/4 reverse*

CREW: *5*

COST: *£220,000*

This heavy rescue vehicle's winch has 90 metres of thick steel cable. It is strong enough to lift something that weighs as much as 15 cars.

MEDTEC SATURN AMBULANCE

Ambulances carry life-saving equipment to accident victims. They rush to the scene and provide emergency treatment to **casualties**. Then they strap them to stretcher beds and take them to the nearest hospital.

DID YOU KNOW?

The first ambulances were bumpy horse-drawn wagons – not a good way to travel if you feel ill! Motorized versions began to appear in the early 1900s.

Some of the Saturn's life-saving equipment is electrically powered. The ambulance carries a poweful **battery pack** to operate this machinery.

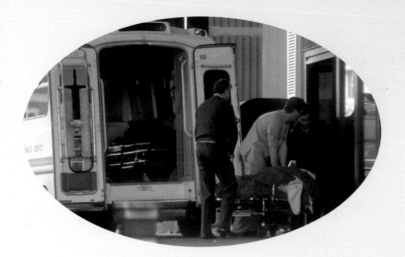

Double rear doors allow stretchers to be loaded easily. The Saturn also has room for over 200 items of equipment.

WATER WITCH EMS
CECIL 793

AMBULANCE

Flashing lights are recognised around the world as the sign of an emergency vehicle.

R44 HELICOPTER

This four-seater helicopter is a police force's 'eye-in-the-sky'. It has lots of special equipment to help them carry out their work. At night, for example, its **infrared camera** allows the police to film what is happening on the ground.

DID YOU KNOW?

The R44 has a special link that lets the crew send live pictures to police on the ground.

Large windows allow clear vision from all of the seats. The **cabin** is also padded out with special foam that reduces **engine** noise.

Helicopters carry less fuel than planes. This means that they can't go as far without stopping. The R44 can go 400 miles on a full **tank** of fuel. This is quite impressive for a helicopter.

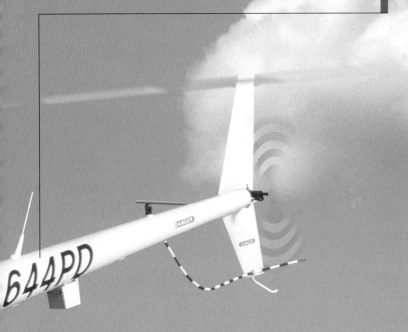

STATS AND FACTS

LAUNCHED: *1993*

ORIGIN: *USA*

MAX POWER: *1,500 bhp*

LENGTH OF HELICOPTER (INC ROTORS): *11.76 metres*

ROTOR LENGTH: *10 metres*

HEIGHT: *3.28 metres*

CRUISE SPEED: *130 mph*

FUEL CAPACITY: *116 litres*

MAX LOAD: *434 kg*

WEIGHT: *654 kg*

MAX FLYING HEIGHT: *4,267 metres*

RANGE: *400 miles*

SPECIAL EQUIPMENT: *Search light, siren, speaker, full-colour and infrared cameras (police version)*

CREW: *2*

COST: *£300,000*

The R44 is made by the Robinson Helicopter Company, based in California. The firm was founded in 1973 by Frank Robinson and now makes more than 300 helicopters each year.

SUPER HUEY HELICOPTER

The Super Huey helicopter was first used by the US army. Then in the 1970s several fire departments in America bought these helicopters. They made changes to them and Super Hueys are now used to control raging forest fires.

DID YOU KNOW?

Huey helicopters were originally called HU-1 Iroquois. The name led to a nickname of 'Huey'.

The Super Huey is quite a large helicopter. There is room on board for a nine-person fire crew and all their firefighting equipment.

When the helicopter has used up its water supply, the pilot will find a water source – a river or lake – to refill its **tank**. The water is sucked up through a **hose**.

STATS AND FACTS

LAUNCHED: *1989*

ORIGIN: *USA*

MAX POWER: *1,100 bhp*

LENGTH: *17.32 metres*

ROTOR BLADE DIAMETER: *14.6 metres*

HEIGHT: *4.08 metres*

MAX SPEED: *138 mph*

FUEL CAPACITY: *916 litres*

MAX LOAD: *2.25 tonnes*

WEIGHT: *2.5 tonnes*

RANGE: *402 miles*

ENDURANCE: *2 hours*

CREW: *9*

COST: *£300,000 (approx)*

The Super Huey has a very large fuel tank. It can carry 916 litres of water and **foam**.

P-3 ORION FIREFIGHTING AIRTANKER

P-3 Airtankers are old military aircraft that have been adapted to carry massive **tanks** of **fire retardant**. These planes are used to help control forest fires. They fill up at airbases, and head for the scene of a fire to drop thousands of litres of retardant on the blaze.

The P-3's pilot tries to drop the fire retardant in a line. This acts as a barrier that stops the fire spreading further.

The P-3's fire-fighting tank is underneath its **body**. It has computer-controlled doors that open to drop the retardant.

DID YOU KNOW?

The Orion is named after a group of stars called Orion, the Great Hunter.

STATS AND FACTS

LAUNCHED (AS AIRTANKER): *1990*

ORIGIN: *USA*

MAX POWER: *2,500 bhp*

LENGTH: *35.6 metres*

WINGSPAN: *30.4 metres*

HEIGHT: *11.8 metres*

MAX SPEED: *411 mph*

RETARDANT TANK CAPACITY: *11,356 litres*

MAX LOAD: *20 tonnes*

WEIGHT: *43.4 tonnes*

MAX TAKEOFF WEIGHT: *63.4 tonnes*

TAKEOFF RUN REQUIRED: *1,300 metres*

CREW: *15*

COST: *£1.5 million*

The P-3 was originally designed as a spy plane. The version that is used for firefighting has low wings and four **turbine engines** with four-blade **propellers**.

FIRE DART FIREBOAT

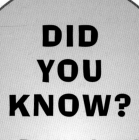
Fireboats are powerful firefighting machines that patrol large harbours and rivers. The Fire Dart works on on the River Thames in London. It is one of the lightest and quickest fireboats ever built.

A jet called a **deck monitor** is used to shoot water in a high stream over a fire. Fire Dart can throw an amazing 1,800 litres of water into the air every minute.

FIRE

There are also teams of fireboats and firefighting **tugs** that tackle large ship fires. These boats draw their water from the sea, so there is no danger of the water running out.

Two massive **engines** power this boat through the water. Together they provide more than 700 **bhp**!

ATLANTIC 75 LIFEBOAT

DID YOU KNOW?

If the boat capsizes, the crew pull a cord to inflate a large airbag. The boat then turns itself the right way up in seconds.

The Atlantic 75 is used to rescue people in trouble up to 50 miles out to sea. This boat is called a **rigid hull inflatable boat**, because it has a glass-reinforced plastic **hull** topped by an **inflatable** tube called a **sponson**.

The hull and sponson are divided into compartments. This means that if one section is pierced, the boat will not sink.

LAUNCHED: *1992*

ORIGIN*: Britain*

MAX POWER: *2 x 70 bhp*

LENGTH: *7.5 metres*

HEIGHT: *0.5 metres*

MAX SPEED: *36.82 mph (32 knots)*

FUEL CAPACITY: *181 litres*

MAX LOAD: *500 kg*

WEIGHT: *1.4 tonnes*

ENDURANCE: *3 hours at max speed*

CREW: *3 person*

COST: *£83,266*

The first rigid hull inflatable lifeboat was designed by the British-based Royal National Lifeboat Institution in the early 1960s. These boats are now used to rescue people all over the world.

The outboard motors are **immersion-proofed**. This means that if the boat capsizes, they start working again as soon as the boat turns the right way up again.

HH-60J JAYHAWK

Air-sea rescue helicopters are used to save people who get into trouble at sea. The pilot holds the helicopter in position while a rescuer is lowered 20 or 30 metres by **winch**. The **casualty** is then rushed off to the nearest hospital. The HH-60J Jayhawk is used by the US Coast Guard.

DID YOU KNOW?

The Jayhawk is based on an old helicopter called the VS-300. Built by Russian-born American engineer Igor Sikorsky, the VS-300 first flew back in 1939.

6566

U.S. COAST GUAR

The small tail **rotor** stops the helicopter from spinning around and keeps it perfectly balanced.

The Jayhawk has a **satellite navigation** system. It tells the pilot exactly where the helicopter is and where to reach people in need of help.

STATS AND FACTS

LAUNCHED: *1986*

ORIGIN: *USA*

MAX POWER: *2 x 1,800 bhp*

LENGTH: *19.81 metres*

ROTOR DIAMETER: *16.46 metres*

HEIGHT: *5.18 metres*

CRUISE SPEED: *160 mph*

MAX SPEED: *300 mph*

FUEL CAPACITY: *2,233 litres*

MAX LOAD: *3.4 tonnes*

WEIGHT: *6.1 tonnes*

RANGE: *700 miles*

SURVIVOR CAPACITY: *6 person*

CREW: *4*

COST: *£10 million*

Each rotor blade is more than 6 metres in length. They can be folded if the helicopter needs to be stored or transported.

LR7 RESCUE SUBMERSIBLE

Perry Slingsby Systems are one of the world's leading makers of rescue **submersibles**. These machines are used to rescue the passengers of submarines that get into trouble. The LR7 is the company's new submersible and will eventually replace the LR5.

The LR7 rescue submersible's rear rescue chamber can hold up to 21 crew and evacuees.

DID YOU KNOW?

The LR7 is fitted with sonar. Sonar uses sound waves to tell the crew where to go in the dark of the deep ocean.

In 2001, the LR5 was used in a attempt to free the crew of a submarine called the *Kursk*. Unfortunately the LR5 arrived too late to help the Russian sailors.

STATS AND FACTS

LAUNCHED: *2004*

ORIGIN: *Britain*

MAX POWER: *10 bhp*

LENGTH: *9.6 metres*

WIDTH: *3.2 metres*

HEIGHT: *3.4 metres*

MAX SPEED: *3 knots (3.5 mph)*

BATTERY CAPACITY: *144 lead acid batteries*

MAX LOAD: *2.5 tonnes*

WEIGHT: *26.5 tonnes*

RESCUE CAPACITY: *18 people plus pilot, co-pilot and medic*

COST: *£4 million (estimated)*

When the LR7 reaches a submarine, it fixes a special section called a transfer skirt onto the escape hatch. When it is fitted securely the trapped passengers can move safely to the LR7.

HAGGLUNDS BV206

This is a Hagglunds BV206 All Terrain vehicle, built in Sweden. It is used for everything from fire fighting to arctic rescue and disaster relief. The BV206 is an amazing vehicle. It even floats, which is very useful when you are travelling over thin ice.

DID YOU KNOW?

The BV206 is also used for desert exploration, jungle exploration and even as a snow taxi for tourists.

Hagglunds BV206's are extremely adaptable vehicles. They can operate in snow, ice, mud, water, grass or sand thanks to their **tracks**.

This all terrain vehicle is made by the German firm Kassbohrer. It rescues people trapped in blizzards and snowdrifts by using a special attachment to shift snow out of the way.

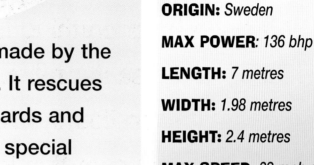

STATS AND FACTS

LAUNCHED: *1994*

ORIGIN: *Sweden*

MAX POWER: *136 bhp*

LENGTH: *7 metres*

WIDTH: *1.98 metres*

HEIGHT: *2.4 metres*

MAX SPEED: *32 mph on roads or 1.86 mph in water*

FUEL CAPACITY: *90 litres*

MAX LOAD: *2.5 tonnes*

WEIGHT: *4.47 tonnes*

CREW: *2*

RESCUE CAPACITY: *10*

COST: *£200,000*

The vehicle's rear car is extremely flexible. It can be converted into an ambulance unit or even into a troop carrier in a matter of minutes.

MARINE PROTECTOR

DID YOU KNOW?

The US Coast Guard has 50 of these boats with 13 more on the way.

This is a Marine Protector Class Coast Guard patrol boat. It is a very fast, strong boat that can operate in rough seas. It is used to stop drug smugglers and chase other criminals. The Marine Protector can also be used for search and rescue missions.

The **pilot house** has lots of special equipment to help the crew. This includes **satellite navigation** and **autopilot**. It also has lots of windows to allow the crew to see in all directions.

U.S. COAST GUARD

A small diesel-powered boat is kept at the back of the patrol boat. It is launched and recovered on a specially designed ramp. Only one person is required on deck for launch and recovery.

LAUNCHED: *1998*

ORIGIN: *USA*

MAX POWER: *5,360 bhp*

LENGTH: *26.5 metres*

WIDTH: *5.18 metres*

MAX SPEED: *28 mph (25 knots)*

FUEL CAPACITY: *11,000 litres*

MAX WEIGHT: *92.4 tonnes*

TOWING CAPABILITY: *200 tonnes*

SURVIVOR CAPACITY: *10*

RANGE: *900 miles*

ENDURANCE: *5 days*

CREW: *10 person*

COST: *£2.2 million*

87325

In America this boat is known as a **cutter**. Cutters are boats more than 19.8 metres in length.

GLOSSARY

AERIAL PLATFORM Platform mounted on the end of a crane's arm.

ARM *See boom.*

AUTOPILOT System that operates a vehicle without a pilot.

BATTERY PACK A portable container that provides the electrical power to make things work.

BHP Brake horse power, the measure of an engine's power output.

BODY Main part of a vehicle that houses the driver and passengers.

BOOM A crane's long, extending arm.

CAB The part of a truck or digger that houses the driver and controls.

CABIN A room in a ship used as living quarters by an officer or passenger, or the part of a plane that houses the pilot and passengers.

CAPSIZE When a boat turns over in the water.

CASUALTY An injured or sick person.

COCKPIT The part of an aircraft where the pilot and his assistants sit.

CRANE A machine for lifting by means of cables attached to a boom.

CUTTER A boat more than 19.8 metres in length.

DECK MONITOR Water jet on a fireboat that shoots water high up into the air.

ENGINE The part of a vehicle where fuel is burned to create energy.

FIRE RETARDANT Liquid dropped onto fires to stop them spreading.

FOAM Frothy substance used to fight fires.

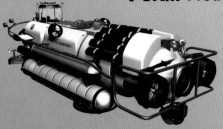

HOSE A tube that carries pressured liquids or gases.

HULL The lower part of a boat.

IMMERSION-PROOFED Protected from water damage.

INFLATABLE A small rubber boat or raft filled with air.

INFRARED CAMERA A camera that can record images at night.

KNOT One nautical mile per hour, equal to 1.15 miles per hour or 1.85 kilometres per hour.

MONITOR A fixed water cannon used to throw a powerful jet of water at a fire.

NOZZLE The end of a hose. Different nozzle attachments result in a different type of water spray, from a mist to a continuous stream.

OUTRIGGERS Feet used to steady a truck.

PILOT HOUSE Part of a ship where the pilot and his controls are based.

PROPELLER A machine with spinning blades that lifts an aircraft off the ground.

PUMP A machine that raises or lifts a liquid or gas.

REMOTE CONTROL The control of an object from a distance.

RIGID HULL INFLATABLE BOAT Boat with a plastic hull topped by an inflatable tube called a sponson.

ROTOR Spinning blade.

SATELLITE NAVIGATON A system which tells you where you are, using satellites in space.

SONAR A system that uses underwater sound waves to detect and locate objects or measure distances.

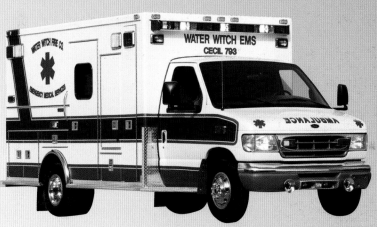

SPONSON An air-filled tube that helps to stabilize a boat on the water.

SUBMERSIBLE A boat that can function under water.

SUBMARINE *See submersible.*

TANK A large container used to store fuel.

TRACKS Two flexible metal loops that help a vehicle to grip on muddy or icy ground.

TUG A powerful boat that pull or pushes ships.

TURBINE Machine with a wheel or rotor driven by water, steam or gases.

WINCH The method of lifting something by winding a line around a reel.

WINGSPAN The distance between the tips of the wings of an aircraft.

INDEX